SCIENTISTS AT WORK

History Detectives
ARCHAEOLOGISTS

Richard and Louise Spilsbury

Heinemann Library
Chicago, Illinois

Design: Richard Parker and Manhattan Design
Illustrations: Darren Lingard
Picture Research: Mica Brancic and Virginia Stroud-Lewis
Production: Alison Parsons

Originated by Modern Age
Printed and bound in China by Leo Paper Group

12 11 10 09 08
10 9 8 7 6 5 4 3 2 1

Library of Congress Cataloging-in-Publication Data

Spilsbury, Richard, 1963-
  History detectives : archaeologists / Richard and Louise Spilsbury.
    p. cm. -- (Scientists at work)
  Includes bibliographical references and index.
  ISBN 978-1-403-49948-6 (hardback : alk. paper) -- ISBN 978-1-403-49955-4 (pbk. : alk. paper) 1. Archaeologists--
Juvenile literature. 2. Archaeology--Juvenile literature. 3. Antiquities--Juvenile literature. 4. Excavations (Archaeol-
ogy)--Juvenile literature. I. Spilsbury, Louise. II. Title.
  CC107.S67 2007
  930.1--dc22
                                   2007012494

Acknowledgments
The publishers would like to thank the following for permission to reproduce photographs: ©Alamy pp. **13**, **18**
(David Hilbert), **7** (Expuesto - Nicolas Randall), **14** (Nick McGowan-Lowe), **22** (Peter Raven/Mark Custance); ©Art
Directors and Trip pp. **9**, **10**, **24**, **26**; ©Bridgeman Art Library p. **19** (Bildarchive Steffens/National Archaeological
Museum, Athens); ©Corbis pp. **5** (Reuters/Aladin Abdel Naby), **11** (Charles O'Rear), **4** (The Art Archive), **6** (Jonathan
Blair), **8** (Ken Cedeno), **15**, **27** (Richard T Nowitz), **12** (Sandro Vannini), **23** (Thorne Anderson); ©Empics p. **25**;
©Getty Images p. **28** (Photodisc); ©Harcourt Education Ltd pp. **21**, **29** (Debbie Rowe); ©Science Photo Library p. **16**
(Adam Hart-Davis); ©The Ancient Art and Architecture Collection p. **17** (R Ashworth).

Cover photograph of human remains in Chapultepec Park, Mexico City reproduced with permission of
©Reuters/Daniel Aguilar.

The publishers would like to thank Patrick Ryan Williams for his assistance in the preparation of this book.

Every effort has been made to contact copyright holders of any material reproduced in this book.
Any omissions will be rectified in subsequent printings if notice is given to the publishers.

Contents

What Do Archaeologists Do? 4

How Do Archaeologists Find Clues? 8

Where Do Archaeologists Study Their Finds? 14

How Do Archaeologists Reconstruct the Past? 20

What Does It Take To Be an Archaeologist? 26

Timeline of Archaeological Discoveries............................28

Glossary...30

Find Out More 31

Index 32

Any words appearing in the text in bold, **like this**, are explained in the Glossary.

What Do Archaeologists Do?

Archaeologists are history detectives! They study human beings, from the recent past all the way back to the first people who walked the planet. Archaeologists work by finding, studying, and interpreting clues from the lives of our ancestors.

Archaeologists help us create a picture of how people lived and what they believed in the past. People lived in houses and wore clothes that were different from the houses and clothing we use today. Archaeologists also help us understand why **cultures**, or knowledge and beliefs of groups of people, have changed over time. For example, new inventions, such as wheels on carts, changed how people moved things around.

These stone knives and axes were made and used by early humans more than 10,000 years ago. They were the most advanced cutting tools people had back then!

Types of archaeologists

Not all archaeologists are the same. Some only study **remains** in specific **environments**. For example, maritime archaeologists search for remains in underwater **shipwrecks**. Some archaeologists study only certain types of clues, such as bones. Zooarchaeologists study the remains of animals kept by people in the past for food or as working animals. Some archaeologists concentrate on specific time periods in history. Egyptologists study remains from the ancient Egyptian culture of roughly 4,000 years ago.

The treasures of Tutankhamen's tomb include his preserved remains and an amazing gold mask.

WHO'S WHO: Howard Carter

Howard Carter was a British Egyptologist who worked in the early 20th century. He started working as an artist who painted Egyptian remains, but later looked for remains himself. Carter became famous worldwide in 1922 when he and his team of assistants found the unopened tomb of the Egyptian pharaoh (ruler) Tutankhamen. It was full of amazing treasures.

Clues

Archaeologists use all types of clues in their work. The most common remains are objects people made to wear, carry, or use. These are called **artifacts**. Artifacts include objects people made, such as clay cooking pots, and objects people found and used, such as sharp animal horns for digging.

Archaeologists often find artifacts that are not whole or are missing pieces, such as a broken toy or bottle. These artifacts may be just as useful for learning about the past as complete ones. Many remains of buildings have been found. These range from a pile of bricks where a house once stood, to complete ancient cities such as Petra in Jordan.

This marine archaeologist is studying artifacts from an ancient shipwreck scattered over the sea floor.

Using words

Do you keep a diary about your life or write about things going on in the world? Historical archaeologists also use what people wrote to learn more about the past. They study words carved into stone, painted on cloth or paper, or printed in old books. Sometimes they even listen to tape recordings of people talking about their lives in the past. This is called oral history. In the future, archaeologists might even study what has been left on our present-day computers.

Historical archaeologists may find useful clues about the past in old books.

WHO'S WHO: Sylvanus Morley

Sylvanus Morley was a 20th century U.S. archaeologist famous for discovering and restoring remains of the Mayan civilization in the jungles of Central America. Morley was inspired in his work by tales of lost cities found by earlier explorers in the region. He was also a spy and an adventurer who showed how exciting archaeological work can be.

How Do Archaeologists Find Clues?

Archaeologists find some remains very easily. More often, though, they must search for artifacts that have been hidden or covered over. They concentrate their work at archaeological **sites**, where there are many remains in one place.

Plowing a field can sometimes uncover archaeological finds.

Finding a site

Over time, clues about the past become hidden. For example, ash and rock from a **volcano** buried the city of Pompeii, Italy. Other ancient Roman sites are now underwater because sea levels have risen since they were built. Sometimes artifacts were buried on purpose and then forgotten about.

Archaeologists often find sites after clues are found at the surface. When old coins are found in a newly plowed field, more artifacts may be nearby. Archaeologists sometimes fly in airplanes to spot unusual shapes in the land. These shapes could lead them to historical sites. For example, a long mound in a flat field could be a burial mound. Others find sites after careful research. They might find a shipwreck after reading about an ancient sea battle. Archaeologists often use tools such as **metal detectors** and **radar** that help them to find things underground.

Starting a dig

Once a site is chosen, a **field crew** of archaeologists and their assistants starts a **dig**. They mark out and measure the area they will search. They create maps to show where any surface features are located.

Archaeologists mark off numbered squares for each dig so that they can easily record the exact spot where they find artifacts.

The science behind it: Radar

Do you know how bats catch flying moths to eat? They make high-pitched squeaks and listen to how the **sound waves** bounce back to find the moths. Radar equipment used by field crews works in a similar way, but uses radio waves. A machine sends radio waves underground. It detects the location of the hidden artifacts when the waves bounce back.

Positioning

The field crew then divides the site into sections using ropes or string attached to pegs. By doing this, they can easily record the section in which the remains are found. A clue is usually much more useful when found in relation to other things. For example, if archaeologists find a few buried wheat grains near the remains of a cooking fire, it suggests that people once spilled wheat as they ate. However, very large numbers of grains in one place could be evidence that ancient people stored food there to survive times when less food grew.

Digging

Digging or **excavation** disturbs archaeological sites. The field crew digs slowly and carefully to make sure that remains are not mixed up, damaged, or destroyed. They mostly use shovels and trowels. Excavation is also carried out carefully to make sure that none of the field crew is injured by falling soil or rock as they dig.

Teams of diggers and heavy equipment are sometimes used by archaeologists to quickly excavate a site after it is uncovered.

Layer by layer

Soil forms in layers. The lowest layers formed first and the surface layers formed last. So a field crew would find remains left by ancient Pueblo Native Americans far beneath more recent Navajo remains, for example. Field crews note the layer in which they find remains and take some soil from it, so they can later determine where the layer fits into the **timeline** of the site.

All artifacts found in a specific layer are usually about the same age.

The science behind it: Identifying soil

Soil layers form naturally when dead plants and animals rot, and as dust in the air or silt in the water builds up on land. People can also create soil layers, such as with the ashes from fires. Different layers often look and feel different. For example, the deeper the layer, the more tightly pressed together the soil. This is because the soil on top is heavy.

Screening the layers

An archaeological dig may involve removing tons of soil, and it would be easy to miss small remains. The field crew has a range of **screens**, which are wooden frames with wire mesh stretched across. They shake or wash soil through the screens to reveal any artifacts.

Archaeologists use brushes to remove dirt from the surface of finds such as this sand mummy in the Valley of the Golden Mummies in Egypt.

TOOLS OF THE TRADE: THE DIG

Here are some tools an archaeologist would find useful:
- Pickaxe/shovel/trowel: for digging
- Bucket/wheelbarrow: to take the soil off the site or to dump it through a screen
- Screens: to separate artifacts from soil
- Brush: to clean artifacts
- Camera/notebook: to record finds
- Clear plastic bags: to organize artifacts
- Kneepads: to protect knees on hard, cold ground
- Glue: to quickly fix accidental breaks of artifacts!

Record-keeping

In order to study a dig and its remains properly, the field crew keeps careful records of their work. Archaeologists use the records to remember what they have seen and found. They do drawings or field sketches, write **field notes**, make maps, and take photographs or videos. These are all important for making sense of their finds later on.

Archaeologists piece together records of the past in much the same way a detective pieces together crime evidence.

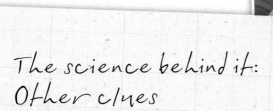

The science behind it: Other clues

Archaeologists study **ecofacts** along with artifacts. Ecofacts are remains of plants and animals that lived at the time of the people who created the artifacts. They include seeds, animal bones, and even the remains of parasites, such as dead fleas. For example, piles of oyster shells might reveal that people ate seafood.

Where Do Archaeologists Study Their Finds?

Digs are only a small part of most archaeologists' work. They often work indoors in **laboratories** and museums, cleaning, studying, and caring for the artifacts they find.

Cleaning

Archaeologists clean up hard remains, such as pieces of broken pottery, using water and old toothbrushes. However, some artifacts, like those made from metal, are damaged by water. For metal objects they scrape off any existing rust and then paint the metal with a special liquid to keep more rust from forming. Groups of metal artifacts found in seawater are often completely rusted together. Archaeologists use tools to separate them before cleaning.

This archaeologist is using a knife to clean an artifact. He may use the magnifying glass to make sure he does not damage the remains.

Sorting

Archaeologists carefully sort out their finds. There is limited space in any collection to store or display artifacts, so they only choose those that are the most important. Archaeologists label the artifacts with the site, site section, and soil layer. They note what the remains are made from and also what they were used for. They may also reassemble broken artifacts from pieces.

This archaeologist is putting together broken pottery found at a cemetery in Israel. She fills in any missing pieces with plaster.

The science behind it: Hard and soft

The remains of people who died centuries ago are mostly hard bones. The skin and tissue has rotted away. Soft skin, flesh, and other materials such as wood, leather, fabric, and paper are **biodegradable**. This means that tiny organisms called **decomposers** in soil, air, or water make them decompose or break down into pieces they can eat. In general, most artifacts and remains found by archaeologists are made of hard materials such as stone, metal, or baked clay. These materials do not biodegrade.

Delicate artifacts

Archaeological finds are often rare and very special, so they need to be protected from damage. For example, scraps of fabrics made by Hopewell Native Americans 2,000 years ago reveal the skill of weavers at that time, the plants they used to make thread, and the colors they dyed their cloth with. Fabrics like this can fade easily or crumble to dust if kept in sunlight, so they are kept in dark places. Archaeologists use special ways of **conserving** artifacts so they don't get ruined. They may spray chemicals on old wooden furniture to kill insects that eat the wood, for instance.

The *Mary Rose* shipwreck is carefully preserved at the Royal Navy Museum in Portsmouth, United Kingdom.

Artifacts recovered from underwater, such as bog bodies (see box) or shipwrecks, can rot if they remain damp. They may shrink, split, and fall apart if they dry out too quickly. Archaeologists sometimes preserve these remains by replacing the water inside them with liquid wax. This process can take a long time. For example, it will take roughly 30 years to preserve the wreck of the *Mary Rose*. This ship was lifted from the seafloor in 1982, more than 400 years after it sank.

Lying in a bog for more than 2,300 years has stained the skin of the Tollund Man, but preserved every detail of his face.

WHO'S WHO: Peter Glob and the Tollund Man

In 1950 archaeologist Peter Glob got a call from police telling him that a body centuries old had been found in a bog in Tollund, Denmark. The body had been perfectly preserved in the bog water, where decomposers cannot survive. Glob discovered that the Tollund Man died more than 2,300 years ago, had fingerprints like those of people today, and that he had eaten barley soup just before he died.

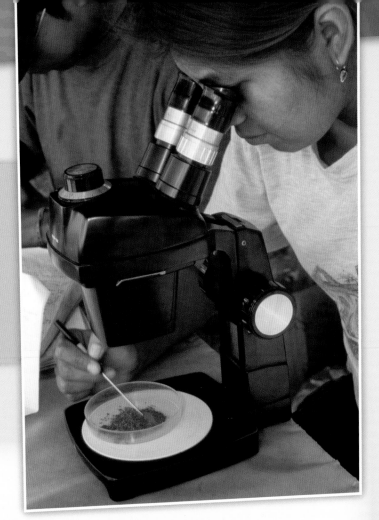

Technology can be an important tool in archaeology. This archaeologist in Mexico is using a microscope to examine seeds from the site of a village that existed in the 700s.

How old?

There are several different ways archaeologists can find out when an artifact was made. The simplest is when a coin or other object has a date on it. Some things were only made at certain times in history. For example, mass-produced, manufactured nails, also called square nails, were first made in the United States in about 1790. So, if archaeologists found square nails at an excavation site, they would know the site was in use after 1790.

Archaeologists date some remains indirectly by **cross-dating**. For example, an arrowhead found in a 500-year-old fireplace is assumed to be the same age. A near identical-looking arrowhead found somewhere completely different could be cross-dated to the same age. Archaeologists can sometimes directly test the age of certain objects. Modern scientific methods to test age directly include **carbon dating** (see box).

Breaking the code

The words on some artifacts are written in ancient languages that use words made up of symbols instead of letters. This means archaeologists must figure out what the symbols mean before they can read about how the people lived. This can take a very long time. It took 20th-century language scholars 50 years to understand the Linear B script, an early form of ancient Greek.

Linear B was found inscribed on this stone tablet now displayed in the National Archaeological Museum in Athens, Greece.

The science behind it: Carbon dating

Most living things and their remains contain carbon **atoms**. One type of carbon atom is called carbon-14. Carbon-14 has a special characteristic. It changes at a regular speed over time and turns into a different type of carbon. Therefore, when scientists examine remains they count how many carbon-14 atoms are left. This number tells them how old the object is. If the remains are of a person, it will tell the scientist how long ago the person died.

How Do Archaeologists Reconstruct the Past?

After conserving their finds, archaeologists figure out what they mean and show others what they have discovered.

Clue experts

Curators are expert archaeologists who care for collections and records of artifacts, ecofacts, and other remains found by archaeologists. They work in museums, historical societies, colleges and universities, and national parks. Curators are often experts on specific periods in history.

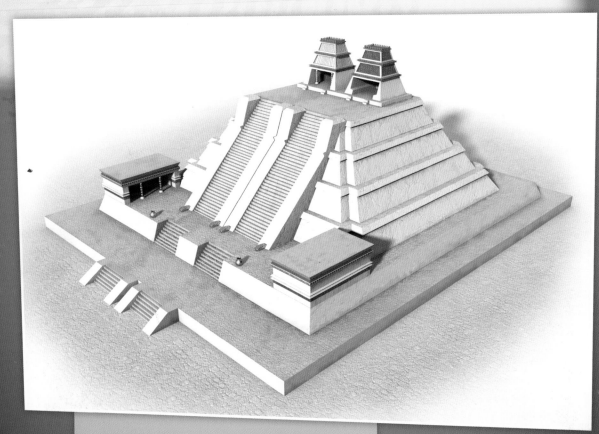

Archaeologists can use computers to recreate how things would have looked in the past, like this Aztec temple.

The terracotta army from Xian, China, has helped people learn a lot about ancient buildings, clothing, and beliefs.

Seeing the past

Archaeologists use their clues to recreate artifacts, buildings, and other remains. They may make models from clay, cardboard, or other materials to show how things may have once looked. Archaeological artists can use skulls they have found and the knowledge they have to **reconstruct** faces in clay. They may also use computers for reconstructions. For example, no complete Iron Age roundhouse, a type of circular hut, exists today. However, computer drawing experts can use special software to create a realistic, three-dimensional view of how the roundhouse looked from different angles.

WHO'S WHO: Terracotta army

Chinese farmers digging a well in 1974 found some life-sized terracotta or red clay figures in the soil. These were the first of more than 8,000 realistic models of soldiers and their horses excavated by archaeologists at the site. They were completed in 208 BCE along with a replica of a Chinese city. The terracotta army was made to protect a Chinese emperor after his death.

Telling the world

Archaeologists usually present the results of a dig in an archaeological report. This adds all the information already known about the site to the new archaeological finds, and explains how the new finds help us understand the past.

Many reports are too complicated for the public to understand. Therefore, archaeologists give lectures and organize exhibitions of artifacts to tell the wider world about their finds. They also publish articles in magazines and write books for the public. Many archaeologists work as professors and teach students how to be archaeologists.

Archaeologists reconstructed this ancient English helmet based on rusty artifacts. They wanted to show the public what it would have looked like 1,500 years ago.

Protection

Archaeological sites are often unique and valuable, so governments make laws to keep them safe. These help to protect sites from accidental damage or from new construction. National and international organizations, such as World Heritage, also help to identify, raise awareness of, and protect sites with great cultural importance. These include the Mesa Verde National Park in the United States and the Great Wall of China. However, some remains have little protection. For example, during the conflict in Iraq that started in 2003, thousands of unique artifacts in museums were looted or stolen to be sold, partly because it wasn't safe to guard them.

These Iraqi artifacts are in safe keeping, but many more artifacts have been looted. Looting in any country removes clues about its history.

WHO'S WHO: Theodore Roosevelt

Theodore Roosevelt became the 26th president in 1901. He made laws protecting wild places and archaeological sites in the United States. Gila Cave Dwellings, New Mexico, became one of the first protected national monuments in 1907. This is a settlement of 40 rooms built into five large caves high up a beautiful sandstone cliff. They were home to the peaceful Mogollon (mug-ee-yone) people roughly 700 years ago.

Archaeologists' lives

Desert dig

The job of an archaeologist can vary from day to day, or month to month. For many archaeologists, their jobs are a mix of fieldwork, research, teaching, and working in the laboratory. They often get to travel around the world in order to carry out fieldwork and meet with other archaeologists. Many archaeologists teach at a university for most of the year, and excavate in the summer.

Dr. Caroline Rocheleau has worked in the hot deserts of Jordan. On a typical day during the excavation, she would normally start work at about 5:00 a.m., before the sun rises and it gets too hot. After spending the morning excavating, she might stop around 1:30 p.m. because of the heat. The afternoons can be spent in the shade, working on the artifacts found in the morning. They need to be cleaned, photographed, and sometimes repaired.

The field crew on a desert dig tries to finish the most tiring work before the hottest part of the day.

Interpreting the past

Archaeologist Amanda Adams, from Minnesota, is a cultural resources manager. This means she helps other archaeologists bring the history of their finds to life for others to enjoy. Spring Lake Park Reserve is a site with 8,000 years of history located on the Mississippi River. Adams helped design its visitor center using artifacts, such as patterns on Native American pottery, for inspiration.

Amateur archaeologists like Kevan Halls have discovered some very exciting artifacts using metal detectors.

WHO'S WHO: Kevan Halls

Kevan Halls is an **amateur** archaeologist. This means he's not a qualified archaeologist, but it is a hobby. For fun he sometimes uses a metal detector to find buried artifacts. In 2000 he found some old gold jewelry in a field near Winchester, England. Archaeologists believe Roman craftspeople made the jewelry, called the Winchester Hoard, more than 2,000 years ago and that it was buried as an offering to the gods.

What Does It Take To Be an Archaeologist?

Inspiration

Are you inspired by the past? Do you like learning about ancient cultures? To learn more, read books about archaeologists or cultures of the past and watch TV shows about famous sites and artifact finds. Visit museums to see ancient treasures and to see reconstructions that bring the past to life.

Visitors to this museum in Denmark can get close to a Viking ship used by people to cross oceans thousands of year ago.

TOOLS OF THE TRADE: HISTORY DETECTIVE SKILLS

Solving puzzles:	you won't always have many clues to work with when piecing together the past
Patience:	field and laboratory work takes time
Sharing:	working and talking ideas through with others helps to understand remains

Taking part

See what archaeologists actually do to help decide whether it is a job you would like. Find out if there is a local archaeological society and go to meetings. Try fun, hands-on activities at archaeological or science fairs. You may even be able to get your hands dirty. Many archaeologists need help from people of different ages to sort through all that soil for artifacts.

These young archaeologists are screening for artifacts.

Study

History lessons are a great way to learn about the past. Studying science will help you learn about bones and conservation of artifacts, and geography helps you understand differences between countries and regions. If you study hard in school, you may be able to go to college to get an archaeology degree. This should help you get a job in archaeology.

Timeline of Archaeological Discoveries

Beginning in the 18th century, thousands of sites and artifacts were discovered, recorded, and interpreted. This was when people first started to seriously study the changes that have taken place in societies since humans first walked the Earth.

1871:
Remains of the city of Troy, mentioned in the famous ancient Greek poem *The Iliad*, are excavated by Heinrich Schliemann

1940:
Four teenagers looking for their dog in southwest France come across the Lascaux cave paintings, some of the oldest paintings on Earth

1747:
Marcello Venuti discovers the Roman city of Pompeii in southern Italy, which was buried by volcanic ash in 79 CE

1911:
The lost Inca city of Machu Picchu is rediscovered by Hiram Bingham

1700s

1800s

1900s

1860:
Farmers in Cambodia tell Henri Mahout about temples in the jungle. Mahout rediscovers Angkor Wat, the capital of the Khmer civilization, abandoned in the 15th century

1891:
Swedish archaeologist Gustav Nordenskiold carries out the first careful collection of artifacts and recorded study of Mesa Verde's Cliff Palace, Colorado

1922:
Tutankhamen's tomb is discovered by Howard Carter

1959:
Peter Throckmorton discovers hundreds of 3,000-year-old sunken ships in the Mediterranean Sea, proving that there was trade between Greece and Turkey

1971:
A set of stone tools used by early humans more than 1.5 million years ago is found by Mary Leakey in Tanzania, Africa

2000:
The Winchester Hoard is found by amateur archaeologist Kevan Halls using a metal detector

2000s >>

1950:
The Tollund Man is excavated and studied by Peter Glob

1967:
Harold Edgerton and John Mills rediscover the remains of the *Mary Rose*, a British battleship

1974:
The terracotta army is found by farmers in central China

2005:
Indian divers find part of the ancient city of Mahabalipuram off the coast of southeast India. It was uncovered after more than 1,300 years by the powerful Indian Ocean tsunami.

Glossary

amateur someone who does something because they enjoy it, not because they get paid for it

artifact remains of a human-made object from the past

biodegradable describes something that decomposes quickly

carbon dating way of determining the age of an object by measuring the proportion of carbon-14 in it

conserve keep from harm or damage

cross-date give an age to something because it is similar to something else of known age

culture way of life of a group of people, such as religion, beliefs, language, and society

decomposer organism such as bacteria that breaks down dead organisms or waste to release nutrients

dig excavation

ecofact natural objects such as seeds or burned wood used but not made by people in the past

environment our surroundings; land, water, and air around us

excavation systematic digging and recording of a site

field crew group of people taking part in a dig

field notes detailed, written notes on excavation and interpretation of a dig

laboratory place where scientists study, conserve, or carry out experiments

metal detector device that uses force of magnetism to find hidden metal objects

radar system that produces radio waves and finds hidden objects by recording how the waves bounce back

reconstruct rebuild or make something to be similar to a lost object from the past

remains artifacts, ecofacts, and other traces of past life

screen sieve with mesh used to separate remains from soil

shipwreck remains of a ship that sank after a battle, storm, or hitting rocks

site place where archaeologists look for artifacts

sound wave invisible vibration passing through a material that can be heard as sound

timeline way of marking historical periods in the order they occurred

volcano opening in ground through which hot, liquid rock from inside the Earth escapes

Find Out More

Further reading

Barnes, Trevor. *Archaeology*. Boston: Kingfisher Books, 2004.

Fagan, Brian. *Archaeologists: Explorers of the Human Past* (Oxford Profiles). New York: Oxford University Press, 2003.

Panchyk, Richard. *Archaeology for Kids: Uncovering the Mysteries of our Past*. Chicago: Chicago Review Press, 2004.

Quigley, Mary. *Dinosaur Digs*. Chicago: Heinemann Library, 2006.

There is an excellent archaeological magazine for children called *Dig*. Visit **http://www.digonsite.com** to find out how to get it. You will also find many links to other interesting archaeological sites.

Websites

Find out about fabulous World Heritage sites near where you live or where you might visit on vacation by clicking on the world map or using the lists of sites at: **http://whc.unesco.org/en/list**

Follow Dr. Dirt, the armadillo archaeologist, on his archaeological examination of a cave in Texas at: **http://www.texasbeyondhistory.net/hinds/kids.html**

Test your knowledge, send in an archaeological picture, or just explore web links to sites and remains around the world at: **http://www.digonsite.com**

There is detailed information about different world cultures with images of interesting artifacts and their uses at: **http://www.carlos.emory.edu/ODYSSEY**

There is information for budding archaeologists on the website of the U.S. Society for Historical Archaeology **http://www.sha.org/students_jobs/default.htm**

Visit the website of the Society for American Archaeology for information about archaeology **http://www.saa.org**

Index

Adams, Amanda 25
amateur archaeologists 25
ancient Roman sites 8
Angkor Wat 28
archaeologists
    becoming an archaeologist
    26-7
    famous archaeologists 5,
    7, 17
    types of archaeologists 5,
    7, 20
    what they do 4
armor 22
artifacts 6, 8, 9, 11, 20, 26, 27
    cleaning 14
    conservation 16, 17
    dating 18, 19
    delicate artifacts 16-17
    screening for artifacts 12, 27
    sorting and labeling 15
Aztecs 20

biodegradable materials 15
bog bodies 17
burial mounds 8

carbon dating 18, 19
Carter, Howard 5
clues about the past 6, 8, 10, 13
coins 8, 18
conservation 16, 17, 27
cross-dating 18
cultural resources managers 25
cultures 4, 26
curators 20

dating 18, 19
decomposers 15, 17
digs 9-13, 14, 22, 24

ecofacts 13, 20
Egypt 5, 12
Egyptologists 5
excavation 10-13

fabrics 16
field crews 9, 10, 11, 13, 24
field notes 13

Gila Cave Dwellings 23
Glob, Peter 17
Great Wall of China 23

Halls, Kevan 25
historical archaeologists 7

information, publicizing 22
Iraq 23
Iron Age roundhouses 21

laboratory and museum work
    14-19, 20
languages, ancient 19
Lascaux cave paintings 28
laws protecting sites 23
Linear B script 19

Machu Picchu 28
Mahabalipuram 29
maritime archaeologists 5, 6
Mary Rose 16, 17, 29
Mayan civilization 7
Mesa Verde National Park 23, 28
metal detectors 8, 25
Morley, Sylvanus 7

Native Americans 11, 16, 25

oral history 7

Pompeii 8, 28
pottery 18, 25

radar 8, 9
reconstructions of the past
    20-1, 26
record-keeping 13
Rocheleau, Caroline 24
Roosevelt, Theodore 23

school and university subjects
    27
ships 16, 17, 26, 29
shipwrecks 5, 6, 8, 17
sites 8, 9, 10, 15, 21, 23, 26
soil layers 11, 15, 18
Spring Lake Park Reserve 25

terracotta army 21, 29
timeline of a site 11
Tollund Man 17, 29
tools, archaeological 8, 12
tools, stone 4, 29
Troy 28
Tutankhamen 5, 28

Viking ships 26

Winchester Hoard 25, 29

zooarchaeologists 5